The Northern Line

A SHORT HISTORY

by

M. A. C. Horne

1987
Published by Douglas Rose
35 Summers Lane, North Finchley, London N12 0PE
but
Distributed by Nebulous Books
12 Raven Square, Alton, Hampshire GU34 2LL

THE NORTHERN LINE

GREAT NORTHERN RAILWAY TO HIGH BARNET

The service between East Finchley and Mill Hill East was opened by the GNR on 22nd August 1867 as part of its Finsbury Park to Edgware line. Finchley (now Finchley Central) to High Barnet followed on 1st April 1872. The GNR was subsequently absorbed by the LNER and London Transport Underground trains were projected on the dates shown here.

GREAT NORTHERN & CITY RAILWAY

The service between Finsbury Park and Moorgate was opened by the GN&CR on 14th February 1904. It was taken over by the Metropolitan Railway on 1st September 1913, and was operated as part of the Northern Line from 1939. The line was closed between Finsbury Park and Drayton Park on 3rd October 1964, between Moorgate and Old Street on 6th September 1975, and between Old Street and Drayton Park on 4th October 1975. British Railways later resumed the service as part of its Great Northern Electrics.

HISTORICAL MAP

Many of the stations on the Northern Line have been renamed since opening; the names shown here are present ones. Readers requiring fuller details are referred to *The London Underground: A Diagrammatic History* also published by Douglas Rose; this shows opening and closing dates and all station name changes for the whole Underground system.

A striking photograph taken from the bottom of the hoistshaft at Stockwell. Looking directly upwards may be noted the underside of the lift used to transfer all the C&SLR rolling stock between depot and track level. To the bottom may be seen the spiral staircase used for staff access. This shaft became disused when Stockwell depot closed and flats were subsequently built on the site. *source UERL official photograph*

To the late Charles E. Lee
a friend I wish I had got to know better
and whose original series of Underground
line histories is the inspiration
for the present work.

The Northern Line: A Short History
by M. A. C. Horne
ISBN 1 870354 00 1
First published in June 1987
© Copyright M. A. C. Horne

The author and publisher wish to acknowledge the assistance of
Printz P Holman, Suzanne Tagg, George Jasieniecki and especially
John Liffen. They are also grateful to the London Transport
Museum for permission to reproduce some of its photographs.

The text in this book has been set in
Linotype Garamond No. 3 10/11pt and 8/8½pt,
with appropriate italic and small caps,
on a Linotron 202/System V.
Typeset by West Farthing Grange, London SW10 9DS.
Cover design by Art Attack, London SW9 6AR.
Printed by Printline Ltd., London EC1R 4RB.

THE NORTHERN LINE is one of the more complicated components of the London Underground system, being an amalgamation of two separately promoted underground electric railways and a section previously part of a main line company. The last expansion of the Northern Line was planned in the 1930s and had it not been for the advent of the Second World War it might have been very much more complicated still. Indeed, evidence of some uncompleted sections can still be seen today.

Below ground level, the oldest part of the Northern Line dates back to 1890 when it opened as part of the City & South London Railway which ran from Stockwell to the City of London. The formal opening took place on 4th November 1890; the ceremony being performed by the Prince of Wales, later to become King Edward VII. The distinguished guests included the Prince's son (the Duke of Clarence and Avondale), the Lord Mayor and Sheriffs of London and many important scientists, engineers and dignitaries. The public had to wait a little longer, the railway opening for passenger traffic on Thursday 18th December 1890.

The opening of the railway heralded the arrival of a new era. It represented the first deep level tube railway in London as well as the first electric railway in London. There were already two other underground railways, the Metropolitan and the Metropolitan District; these made use of steam haulage. Many of the sections of these two Lines operated in open air and were similar to other railways of the day. Even in the central area where tracks ran in tunnel the stations were frequently in the open. The City & South London was quite different. On entering the station the passengers paid a flat fare of twopence through a booking office window and made their way through paygates, as they were called, into hydraulic lifts which took them down to the lower levels. On reaching the platforms passengers found the station tunnels finished with brilliant white tiling, to try and make best use of the permanent artificial light, initially provided by gas lamps.

The low, squat trains consisted of three carriages, entrance to which was gained by gated vestibules between them, each manned by a uniformed conductor who would also call out the names of the stations along the route. There were no windows as such in the carriages and the upholstery of the seatbacks was carried almost up to roof level, leaving narrow glazed slits; these carriages quickly became known as 'padded cells' as a result. The trains were hauled by diminutive four-wheeled locomotives each with a pair of motors, one mounted directly on each axle. When the Line opened a five minute service was provided each way and during the remaining eleven days to the end of the year a phenomenal 165,000 passengers were carried, reflecting a considerable level of public curiosity (numbers then

A drawing (probably none too accurate) of a C&SLR paygate and fare window arrangement taken from the official brochure produced at the time of the railway's opening.

source M A C Horne Collection

dropped, averaging about 93,000 per week during the next half year but rising slightly thereafter).

Although opened in 1890 the railway had been a long time in coming. It was largely the result of the activities of three men, Peter William Barlow, James Henry Greathead (one of Barlow's pupils) and Charles Grey Mott, who became chairman of the company which constructed the line.

Barlow was principally a railway engineer; however, he became involved in the design of the former Lambeth suspension bridge opened in 1863 and built under his direction. Part of the construction of this bridge involved the sinking of cast-iron cylinders into the river bed to form pier foundations. It occurred to Barlow that cast-iron tunnels of similar construction could just as easily be driven horizontally under the river with perfect safety, and he subsequently advocated that such tunnels could be used as "omnibus subways for the relief of traffic congestion in London".

Barlow proposed a method of construction involving the use of a circular shield used to protect men boring the tunnels; as each shield was pushed forward, and the earth excavated, the resulting tunnels would be lined immediately with cast-iron segments. Such a tunnel could be driven easily within the London clay and sufficiently deeply to avoid interfering with the pipes and sewers of the public utilities which ran just below street level. Because of the depths involved lifts, rather than stairs, would be necessary for passenger access.

Inspired by these thoughts Barlow obtained parliamentary powers in 1868 for construction of a subway under the Thames near the Tower of London. In 1870 he obtained powers for a second subway from the City, near London Bridge, to St George's Church, Southwark. The Tower Subway was built fairly quickly in 1869 under Greathead's direction. He undertook the task because contractors were unenthusiastic to become involved with shield tunnelling after many difficulties with Brunel's Thames Tunnel at Rotherhithe, even though the latest proposal was in practice quite different. The Tower Subway opened in 1870 using a cable-hauled car, but it was not a financial success and soon closed. This unpromising start influenced the second scheme, known as the Southwark & City Subway, which was abandoned.

Although not financially viable the Tower Subway had given Greathead a certain amount of experience in construction of iron lined tube tunnels and suggested various technical improvements which could be made. For this reason he became involved in later reviving and extending the Southwark & City proposal, and in 1884 powers were obtained for the construction of a tube railway from the Monument to Elephant & Castle; this Act, the City of London and Southwark Subway Act, again envisaged the use of cable-hauled carriages. In 1887 an extension of the subway from Elephant & Castle to Stockwell was authorized, to make better use of the traffic potential.

Tunnelling actually started in October 1886. Work commenced from a shaft constructed from the Old Swan Pier, just upstream of London Bridge. By the following June the river tunnels were completed without major problems arising – this was regarded as the most difficult part of the scheme. The rest of the line was then constructed from shafts sunk at the Monument, St George's Church, Elephant & Castle, Kennington, the Oval and Stockwell, and by the end of 1890 the pioneer tube railway was ready for operation. Trouble was experienced with some of the tunnelling when water-bearing ground was encountered. The idea was adopted of excavating such sections with the miners working in compressed air – the first occasion when tunnels were built with a shield under such conditions.

Although cable haulage had been proposed as the system of propulsion the company became increasingly worried about the considerable operating difficulties which were likely to occur, and they looked with interest at the few pioneer electric systems then in operation. After much investigation the company was persuaded to employ Messrs Mather & Platt as electrical contractors, their chief engineer, Dr Edward Hopkinson, having had much experience with pioneer electrical traction on the Bessbrook & Newry Tramway in Ireland. John Hopkinson (Edward's brother) was employed as consulting engineer for the project. From 1888 the subway company took the necessary steps to facilitate the use of electrical traction, the decision being confirmed after successful experimental running took place in 1889. However, the initial proposal for cable haulage, and certain construction expediences, meant that some parts of the new line were not entirely suitable for the use of electric locomotives, restrictive tunnel diameter, sharp curves and steep gradients being the major difficulties. Nevertheless the line opened under the revised name of the City & South London Railway (C&SLR) as the first major electric railway in England.

The stations on the new line were at King William Street (near the Monument), Borough, Elephant & Castle, Kennington, Oval and Stockwell, and the line was about 3½ miles (5·6km) from end to end. Apart from King William Street where an existing building was adapted, the remaining stations were of an attractive design by T P Figgis and each incorporated a large dome above the lift shaft. The depot was at Stockwell, just east of the Clapham Road, and

A drawing of Oval station taken from the C&SLR opening brochure. It is fairly typical of the original stations by T P Figgis, the most prominent feature being the dome housing the equipment for the hydraulic lifts. Most of the early stations have been extensively rebuilt although Kennington is relatively unspoilt and still retains the lift dome.

source M A C Horne Collection

consisted of carriage and locomotive sheds and sidings. This was connected to the railway by a long inclined tunnel at the steep gradient of 1 in 3½ and up which the trains were hauled by a rope. In later years this tunnel went out of favour, notably after a train ran away, and was replaced by a large lift which brought the locomotives and carriages to the surface one at a time. To ease matters, a complex of sidings was built at the lower level and some maintenance was done there without the need to bring the carriages to the top level.

The power station was also built at Stockwell and comprised three Edison-Hopkinson dynamos powered by 375hp Fowler Engines. It should be recalled that large scale electricity generation was very much in its infancy in London and not only was Stockwell the first to supply a traction load but was, when opened, the largest generating plant in the city. No substation plant was provided, the power being fed directly to the single conductor rails which lay between the running rails of each track (though not in the centre because of clearance problems). Because the railway was fed only at the southern end there could be a substantial voltage drop at the City end and this occasionally became a problem on the steeply inclined approach to

King William Street; contemporary reports suggest that not all trains managed to get up this incline at the first attempt and that even on those which did the lighting in the carriages faded to a dim red glow. The power station and electrical equipment were installed by Mather & Platt Limited of Manchester, and most of the credit for its success must rest with the consulting engineer, John Hopkinson.

The up and down lines were carried in separate cast-iron tunnels which, north of Elephant & Castle were only 10ft 2ins (3·1m) in diameter — this was a legacy of the plan for cable traction where a 10mph cable was proposed on this section, demanding only minimal clearance. South of Elephant & Castle, it had been proposed to use a 12mph cable and a slightly more generous clearance was offered, the tunnels being 10ft 6ins (3·2m) in diameter.

The stations at Stockwell and King William Street consisted of a single, large-diameter tunnel — at Stockwell a platform flanked by two tracks and at King William Street a single track with a platform either side. The other stations each had a separate tunnel for each track. All station tunnels were of brick construction and were not circular, the lower portion being flattened off in a manner similar to many large brick railway tunnels. These tunnels were generally about 200 feet (about 61m) long.

The early train service was restricted by several factors: the limited power supply, the arrangement of block signalling from station to station, and the need to change locomotives at the terminal stations. These locomotives, 14 originally, were built by Mather & Platt. A form of control known as series/parallel control was adopted (patented by John Hopkinson in 1887) with accelerating resistances being switched out by a hand controller. The Westinghouse air brake system was used but the locomotives were not provided with air compressors to supply the braking system; the reservoirs had therefore to be recharged once on every round trip at Stockwell. At the opening of the line there were 30 coaches built by the Ashbury Carriage & Wagon Company, which seated 32 people each.

During the next few years a number of shortcomings were discovered and overcome as traffic increased. Seven further locomotives were constructed by various manufacturers in the period to 1899; these bore certain differences to the first batch although substantially similar. 54 further coaches were delivered during the same period, once again very similar but incorporating proper windows (later at least some of the padded cells were reconstructed to incorporate windows). The power supply was also improved by installing a fourth Edison-Hopkinson dynamo, and by further re-arrangements in 1895 and 1896. The line capacity was further improved by the introduction of additional signals which allowed the block sections to be shortened.

The signalling system was essentially of a mechanical nature, although with a novel form of 'Lock and Block' control superimposed where an electrical detector proved a train to have left the section before the following one could be signalled forward. Signal cabins were provided at all stations and at Borough, Kennington and Oval the differences in platform level meant a separate cabin was needed on each platform. One of the more significant adjustments made was the alteration of the wholly inadequate layout at King William Street to an island platform with a track each side. Although this increased capacity and allowed an improved level of service it further shortened the platform length and made it difficult to run trains longer than three coaches. Arrangements were then pursued vigorously to abandon this station and build a new line through to the City which avoided these problems. In order to improve operation experiments were also made with a 4-coach 'motor-coach' train – no separate locomotives being used. However, the train operated not entirely without difficulty and the idea was dropped after the King William Street re-arrangements.

Powers had been obtained in 1893 for a northward extension of the line to Islington. As executed, the works involved the construction of new tube tunnels from a point just north of Borough station; these tunnels ran fairly close to the existing alignment to a point near to the London Bridge station of the South Eastern Railway, where a new C&SLR station was constructed with interchange facilities, and then continued beneath the river to new stations at Bank (interchange with the soon to open Central London Railway) to terminate temporarily at Moorgate Street.

The new portion of the line opened on Sunday 25th February 1900. Each of the three new stations was constructed in twin large-diameter cast-iron tunnels, lined with white tiles, and access from the surface to lower levels was achieved by means of electric lifts. At

City & South London Railway locomotive number 10 in the depot at Stockwell. This locomotive was involved in the opening ceremony in 1890 and was given the name *Princess of Wales*, although this was only painted on the side panels. The later batches were similar, the most noticeable difference being the design of the side panels which were flared out at waistrail level. *source M A C Horne Collection*

A contemporary wash drawing illustrating the station at King William Street (C&SLR) in the period 1890-95. The platform on the left is used for departure traffic and the other for those arriving. The layout was adjusted such that in the period from 1895 until closure in 1900 there were two tracks with a single island platform between.

source London City Leadenhall Press (1891)

Bank the company constructed a sub-surface ticket hall for which purpose they acquired the crypt of St Mary Woolnoth church. In the event it became necessary for massive underpinning work to be done as the fabric of the church was found to be less substantial than originally thought. Although the work was eventually completed with entire technical satisfaction it became necessary for the sum of £17,000 to be paid to the church authorities by way of compensation, though not until the railway had unsuccessfully contested this in the House of Lords. The new surface station at Moorgate Street was a fairly impressive building and when the extension opened the company removed their office there. The link to King William Street was abandoned. Although powers had been obtained as long previously as 1890 for an extension south to Clapham, it had not been expeditious for it to be built so long as the City bottleneck had existed. With the prospect of the Moorgate extension looming, the Clapham extension at last became viable and work commenced in 1898. Two new stations were built, Clapham Road (now Clapham North) and Clapham Common. The platform tunnels at both con-

Exterior of a train of 1902 coaches for the C&SLR built by G F Milnes & Company

source M A C Horne Collection

sisted of a single 29ft 8ins (about 9m) diameter tunnel with an island platform flanked by the two tracks. Again, electric lifts connected the lower station levels with the new surface buildings. The extension came into use on 3rd June 1900.

Once the former City terminus had been jettisoned it became possible to start operating 4-coach trains with immediate traffic relief. The Stockwell power house and the power supply systems were totally unsuitable for the expanded railway and a new power house was built nearby with a capacity of 3·25 megawatts, the former building being converted to repair shops. A 5-wire distribution system was adopted (another invention of John Hopkinson) with 2000 volts between the outer conductors, and with 1000 volts between the inner conductors; a substation was provided at London Bridge. This arrangement caused the conductor rails on each track to be opposite polarities to each other, one being 500 volts above and the other 500 volts below, earth. Balancers and storage batteries maintained these voltages during periods when an unequal load was being drawn on either track. Further locomotives and coaches were purchased to furnish the two extensions and some of the older locomotives were rebuilt and modernized. Coaches were similar in principle to the older batches, though detailed changes, to the windows for example, were made; wooden construction on a steel underframe continued. The turnstile method of payment was also superseded by a graduated fare system using tickets.

The remainder of the Islington extension, north of Moorgate, opened on 17th November 1901 with an intermediate station at City Road. The latter station was built with separate platform tunnels while the Islington station, called Angel, was built with an island platform in a single large diameter tunnel. A further substation was built at Angel. Electric lifts were provided at both stations. By the time this extension was opened the locomotive stock had risen to 52 and the coaching stock to 124, increasing to 132 the following year. Traffic had increased very considerably by this time, nearly 13½ million being carried in 1901 compared with just over 5¼ million in 1891.

Interior of 1902 coach for the C&SLR built by G F Milnes & Company

source M A C Horne Collection

The final extension of this railway, while still an independent concern, was in 1907 when it pushed farther north to tap the main line traffic at King's Cross, St Pancras and Euston. The extension opened on 12th May 1907 with the terminal station, Euston, consisting of the usual island platform layout in a single large tunnel and the intermediate station, King's Cross St Pancras, comprising two separate tunnels. King's Cross was unusual in that the platform level was served directly by the new electric Otis lifts, although the booking hall was below street level. At Euston a particularly ornate station building was erected in Eversholt Street although a second booking hall, shared with another new tube, the Charing Cross, Euston & Hampstead Railway, was constructed beneath part of the main line station of the London & North Western Railway. Each booking hall had its own separate electric lifts which led to opposite ends of the new platform. Between Angel and King's Cross an intermediate signal cabin was required and a subterranean cabin with surface access from Weston Street (now Weston Rise) was provided, together with a dip in each track to assist trains to restart – still detectable today. A further 33 coaches were provided to service the extension, this time of steel-bodied construction but otherwise generally similar to their predecessors; by now 165 carriages had been built and all trains were operated as 5-coach sets. A novel feature at Euston was the provision of an engine traverser in a connecting tunnel just north of the station, to aid the process of locomotives running round.

The second underground railway component of the Northern Line also opened in 1907 and was called the Charing Cross, Euston & Hampstead Railway (CCE&HR), operating from a station beneath Charing Cross (South Eastern) Railway to Golders Green, with a branch from Camden Town to Highgate (now called Archway).

The origins of this line go back to the success of the City & South London Railway; following its inauguration in 1890 several new tube railway schemes were promoted and the Hampstead, St Pancras & Charing Cross Railway Bill was just one of various tube railway bills presented to the 1892 parliamentary session. It contemplated a railway between the junction of the High Street and Heath Street at Hampstead, via Haverstock Hill, Chalk Farm Road and Camden Town, thence Hampstead Road, Tottenham Court Road and Charing Cross Road to a station at the junction of Strand and Southampton Street. A branch was proposed diverging northwards at the Euston Road and running under Drummond Street to Euston and King's Cross. Stations were proposed at Hampstead, Belsize Park, Chalk Farm, Camden Town, Seymour Street, Euston Road, Oxford Street, Charing Cross and King's Cross.

Parliament established a committee to examine the Bills and after full deliberation it reported favourably and the Bill received the Royal Assent on 24th August 1893 – although the railway had become known as the Charing Cross, Euston & Hampstead Railway in the meantime and the section from Euston to King's Cross had been dropped east of Chalton Street.

Difficulty was found in procuring the necessary share capital and the directors had to be content with keeping the scheme alive rather than in actual construction. Powers were renewed in 1897, and in 1898 a further Act substituted a new southern terminus beneath Craven Street instead of Strand/Southampton Street. In 1899 another Act diverted the main line along Eversholt and Seymour Streets instead of the Hampstead Road, thus placing Euston station on the main line instead of a branch. This Act authorized a new branch line from Camden Town to Kentish Town (Midland) railway station and thence to a depot and power station a little farther north. By now electric operation was clearly intended although when first mooted it was felt that the gradients would demand cable haulage. Powers were again renewed in 1900 but despite numerous attempts the capital was still not forthcoming.

Matters soon took a remarkable turn. Various American businesses had been establishing themselves in areas of British industry as a result of their own domestic expansion losing impetus. One such businessman, heavily involved in the American tramway industry, became interested in the dormant CCE&HR and purchased the powers for the line on 1st October 1900. The man was Charles Tyson

Yerkes, of Chicago, who claimed to have backing worth 30 million pounds and the vision to see how London could be transformed by the provision of frequent electric railway services between the suburbs and the centre of town – and the vision to see how such services could produce the necessary reward for his syndicate. But Yerkes did not stop at the CCE&HR. He took the opportunity to acquire a controlling interest in the ailing Metropolitan District Railway which was a steam operated sub-surface underground railway suffering from the effects of competition. It was his intention to modernize and electrify the line to restore its fortune. He also acquired control of a partly built tube – the Baker Street & Waterloo Railway (BS&WR) and the powers for two further tube schemes which he amalgamated into the Great Northern, Piccadilly & Brompton Railway (GNP&BR). Yerkes established a holding company on 15th July 1901 known as the Metropolitan District Electric Traction Company Limited; this was reconstituted on 9th April 1902 as the Underground Electric Railways Company of London Limited (UERL). Work on tunnelling the CCE&HR started in September 1903 – after yet further changes had been sanctioned by Parliament on 18th November 1902. This authorized a novel extension beyond Hampstead to the pastures of Golders Green in the face of much opposition by those who thought the line would ruin the Heath. It had another benefit of considerably easing the gradients between Chalk Farm and Hampstead. A new depot and power station site was also authorized near Golders Green (although a site in Hampstead had been authorized in the original Act) and the branch line was extended northwards to a point near the Highgate station of the Great Northern Railway via an intermediate station at the bottom of Highgate Hill – this station, now called Archway, opened as Highgate and the portion, beyond, to Highgate (GNR) was not proceeded with.

The UERL acted as the main contractor for the three subsidiary tube companies, as a result of which common standards and a common style were adopted so far as possible. One of the most interesting features of the method of construction is that it was entirely in the hands of a team of American specialists, hand-picked for their expertise by Yerkes and accompanying him from the USA in 1900. Construction was supervised from the Chief Draughtsman's office at Hamilton House, on the Embankment – a building which still stands. Much of the UERL's ideas were thus based on then current American practice, a point which cannot be overemphasised. It is interesting that when their task was complete most of the team returned to the USA, although Yerkes himself did not live to see any of the tube schemes open. It was a bone of contention at the time that so much of the equipment used on the railway also came from the USA, despite assurances to the contrary. For example, the steel rails were shipped across the Atlantic. The rolling stock was also American and it was said at the time that the delivery period for similar British built stock was too long – not, perhaps, an unfamiliar sentiment today!

Subcontractors for the CCE&HR tunnelling were Price & Reeves and the company made use of a Price rotary excavator – a power-driven excavator associated with a tunnelling shield – which was capable of driving 96 rings (160 feet – about 49m) a week. Greathead shields were used on difficult portions. The internal diameter of the running tunnels was 11ft 8¼ins (about 3·56m). Station tunnels were built to an internal diameter of 21ft 2½ins (about 6·46m) and, unlike the C&SLR, all station platforms were built in separate tunnels.

Tunnelling work was completed in December 1905 and activities turned towards equipping the line. A station which had proved a special problem was Charing Cross, the terminus. The station lay beneath the South Eastern Railway station, which latter company objected to any work liable to interfere with road traffic access to its forecourt; as a result the CCE&HR were forced to contemplate constructing their lift shafts from the bottom upwards, to the level of the booking hall beneath the forecourt. However, a devastating accident where the arched roof of the main line station collapsed rendered the station closed and the forecourt free for the CCE&HR to use; an agreement was quickly reached between the two companies and in the remarkably short time of six weeks the surface was excavated, the side walls of the booking hall were built and roofed over with girders and one of the lift shafts was excavated to its full depth – the remaining shaft being dug later from the covered booking hall.

The new railway opened for public traffic on 22nd June 1907, a Saturday, although still not quite complete in all details and thus remaining in the hands of the contractors for some weeks more. David Lloyd George, then President of the Board of Trade and having previously opened the associated GNP&B railway, agreed to open the CCE&HR and took a further opportunity to try his hand at driving a train using an engraved golden key with which he was subsequently presented. A formal luncheon was held at Golders Green in the depot paint shop where the main dignitaries entertained their fellows with the customary speechmaking. Meanwhile the railway opened its gates to the public, and amid a blaze of publicity made no charge for the privilege of sampling its stations and services for the rest of the day. It was estimated that between 120 and 150 thousand passengers made use of this offer.

The CCE&HR was about 8 route miles (about 13km) long at the time of opening, including the branch to Highgate. Sixteen stations were provided, all except Golders Green giving access to twin plat-

A magnificent photograph by Harry Bedford Lemere of the station at Mornington Crescent, entirely typical of Leslie Green's exterior design of all stations on the CCE&HR except Golders Green. Where the design allowed, as in this case, the lifts deposited passengers directly into the street, and on corner sites the entrance was usually in a different face of the building. Lift equipment was housed in the upper floor and the roof of the buildings were flat to allow for future commercial development.   *source National Monuments Record*

forms by means of electric lifts provided by the Otis Elevator Company, the number of lifts varying between two and five according to the traffic anticipated. The platforms at Golders Green were in the open air and on an embankment; a central 'departure' platform was located between the two tracks and a pair of 'arrival' platforms was provided on the flanks. A brick station building was constructed which connected with subways leading to flights of stairs for arrival and departure traffic.

At all other stations except Charing Cross and Oxford Street the station buildings were two-storey, steel-framed constructions clothed in ruby-red terracotta. Although the buildings all differed in detail a fairly uniform appearance was achieved. At ground floor level a ticket office was provided in the area leading to the lifts and at first floor (or mezzanine) level the lift machinery was installed. At Oxford Street and Charing Cross the ticket halls were beneath street level and access was provided by steps or sloping subway. Lift machinery rooms were not possible above the lifts at those two stations because no clearance was available and they had to be placed at the bottom of

A train of 1907 ACF 'gate' stock photographed outside the depot at Golders Green. The gated platforms at the end of the cars (the only means of access) are clearly visible.

source UERL official photograph

the lift shafts. The deepest shaft was at Hampstead where the lift travel was 183 feet (56m), and the shallowest Chalk Farm, which was 30 feet (9m).

The lower station levels were all similar in that separate routes were provided to and from the lifts and each platform. The platforms were about 350 feet (about 107m) long. The walls were covered in tilework designed to a common theme consisting of basically white or cream background divided vertically at intervals by bands of coloured tiles carried up and over the plasterwork ceiling vault, giving the tunnel a curiously barrel-like appearance. Between the bands were three horizontal sets of coloured tiles, between the middle and upper pair of which were decorative arrangements in *Art-Nouveau* style. Some of the resulting panels instead carried the station name which was fired into the tilework. The architect responsible for all the station's was Leslie W Green, and the resulting tilework designs meant that each station presented a unique combination of pattern and colour – a similar scheme had been employed on the two associated tube railways where common standards had been adopted.

The construction of the cars (an American term) was largely in steel, partly to minimise the fire hazard, and the internal finish comprised non-flammable mahogany. The electrical equipment was constructed by the British Thomson-Houston Company to American (GEC) specifications and was based on the multiple-unit system of control devised by Sprague, which had proved very successful on the Central London Railway. The two traction motors on the motor cars were each rated at 200hp. The braking system consisted of the well-established Westinghouse air brake.

Rolling stock was delivered to Golders Green by road and numbered 150 cars built by the American Car & Foundry Company in the USA and shipped over and assembled in Manchester. Sixty of the cars were motor cars, provided with a driving cab, single motor-bogie and an equipment compartment mounted over the motor-bogie. The

Interior of a 1907 ACF motor car looking towards the driving end. The Hampstead Line diagram beneath the roof clearly dates the picture as post 1914 and shows how Charing Cross (on the loop line) was shown.   *source UERL official photograph*

remaining cars were unpowered, 50 (known as control trailers) having a driving position and 40 (trailers) without. They were painted a rich maroon colour described as Midland Lake and carried the initials of the company and fleet number in blocked gold lettering. Trains were initially of five cars but three cars were stabled at quiet times leaving a two-car portion (motor and control trailer) in service.

Power derived from the main generating station at Lots Road, which provided power to the District Railway and all three UERL tube lines. The southern end of the CCE&HR was fed directly from the District Railway substation at Charing Cross, which also fed the Baker Street & Waterloo. Additional substations were built at Euston, Belsize Park, Golders Green and Kentish Town – in each of these four a pair of rotary converters was installed to convert the 11,000 volts, three phase, a.c. supply to 550 volts d.c. for feeding the conductor rails. The high tension feeders and the 550 volt supply from Charing Cross substation were connected to Charing Cross (CCE&HR) station through a cable tunnel along the length of Villiers Street.

Signalling was, where possible, completely automatic and operated by electrical track circuits to detect the presence of trains. The signals consisted of a moving spectacle plate containing red and green aspects which occluded an oil (later electric) lamp – the spectacle being moved by compressed air controlled by an electric valve in accordance with the presence of a train ahead. In addition, an air-operated 'trainstop' lever afforded protection against a train passing a signal at danger. The lever arm was inclined upwards when the sig-

19

nal showed red and would engage with a lever on a passing train to apply the emergency brakes. When a signal showed green then the trainstop lever was depressed clear of the passage of trains. Signal cabins were provided at Charing Cross, Mornington Crescent, Camden Town, Highgate, Hampstead and Golders Green owing to the presence of pointwork and crossovers. Westinghouse electro-pneumatic lever frames were installed with miniature levers to control points and associated signals. At Golders Green, in the open air, pneumatically controlled lower quadrant semaphore signals were erected.

The opening of the Charing Cross, Euston & Hampstead Railway not only completed Yerkes's planned scheme but represented the end of underground railway development through central London. Until this point the deep level electric lines had been considered to be short, high density, urban concerns with trains at relatively frequent intervals running from end to end of the lines. From this point onwards the enthusiasm for similar lines vanished for over sixty years and the CCE&HR's own description of itself as *The Last Link* was more final than was perhaps envisaged at the time. Subsequent development relied upon exploiting the residual spare capacity of the already built tube lines (though perhaps at the cost of comfort) by expansion outwards and creating much new traffic by opening up rural and previously unserved areas. Over the next forty years the character of these early tube lines therefore changed dramatically and themselves strongly influenced the development and shape of what has become Greater London.

The new railway settled down to a stable existence. The inconvenience of the station naming in the West End was soon acknowledged, particularly at Oxford Street with its busy interchange with the Central London's Tottenham Court Road station, and the latter name was adopted in 1908. As a result the CCE&HR's existing station of that name became Goodge Street on the same date. The following year Euston Road became Warren Street.

Shortly after opening the process of operation in concert with the other UERL tubes developed markedly. A common rule book was adopted, company passes became interchangeable, common conditions of service applied, rolling stock was interchanged between lines as necessary, and the lines became 'marketed' as one. From 1909 agreement was reached between the UERL companies and the independent Central London, City & South London, Great Northern & City and Metropolitan Railways for the joint use of the word UNDERGROUND with large initial and final letters and a narrow bar above and below the other letters. This was applied to station entrances to promote a common image and at about the same time a joint map was produced for use on the respective companies' publicity.

The interdependence of the three UERL tubes was officially recognised in 1910 when the GNP&B Railway was renamed the London Electric Railway (LER) and absorbed the BS&W and CCE&H Railways. This allowed some further economies and full pooling of receipts between the three components. Thereafter, the former CCE&HR became most widely known as the Hampstead Line (although initially the term Hampstead Tube was used). The next most significant development was the acquisition by the UERL of the Central London and City & South London Railways in 1913; while both railways retained a fully independent legal existence they were gradually stripped of many physical manifestations of independence and were required to conform as far as possible to UERL practice. This was not an easy thing to do in the case of the C&SLR which had to contend with the problems of being a pioneer, already being somewhat old-fashioned after twenty-three years of operation. An early move was to close the power station at Stockwell and take power from Lots Road instead. Through bookings and tickets, publicity and staff training were standardized with UERL practice quickly too.

In 1914 a pooling system was adopted between all the UERL companies to spread the load of investment and revenue between lines. A proposal was soon made for the physical connection of the C&SLR with the Hampstead Line and the entire replacement of the C&SLR rolling stock with multiple-unit equipment, but there were more pressing matters in 1914 and it was not considered further until after the First World War. Something which was celebrated that year was an extension of the Hampstead Line to Charing Cross (Embankment) station by means of a single platform on a large reversing loop (Charing Cross, Hampstead Line, station being renamed Charing Cross (Strand) on the same day). The loop was constructed from a working shaft in Embankment Gardens and was 880 yards (805m) in length. The platform was linked to a new concourse beneath the District Railway platforms by means of a pair of escalators (the first on the Hampstead Line) and a lengthy subway provided interchange between the Hampstead and Bakerloo Lines at low level. In 1915 Charing Cross (Embankment) became simply Charing Cross and Charing Cross (Strand) became Strand — a not wholly satisfactory solution to a rather difficult problem not finally resolved until 1979.

A move of rather more doubtful benefit in 1914 was a concentration of booking facilities at Euston. When opened, both the CCE&HR and C&SLR companies constructed their own surface structures which provided independent lift access to their respective platforms. In addition there was joint booking office and lift access beneath the LNWR main line station, this latter company owning the freehold and requiring as a term of the agreement the two underground railways to maintain their own independent stations. In 1914 this agreement was altered and the two separate surface stations were closed – in due course the C&SLR station was demolished and the CCE&HR station used to incorporate a much enlarged substation. The main line access survived amid unhappy congestion until 1967 when it was superseded by more adequate arrangements.

After the war the Government sought to reduce the unemployment problem by encouraging expenditure on capital schemes and in 1921 passed the Trade Facilities Act which provided for a Treasury guarantee for borrowed investment. The UERL was quick to take advantage of the agreement and put together a scheme based on several pre-war projects which were planned or partly started. One part of the scheme was the fulfilment of a twenty year old plan to extend the Hampstead Line to Edgware. An independently promoted railway had been floated in 1901 to form a junction with the CCE&HR at Hampstead, running beneath the Heath and thence via Hendon to Edgware. After wrangling with the CCE&HR, who intended a parallel line beneath the Heath as far as Golders Green, and in an attempt to placate those interested in the Heath's preservation, it was agreed that Yerkes would assume control of the Edgware & Hampstead Railway (E&HR) and that the junction with the CCE&HR would be made at Golders Green. The E&HR thus became a part of the UERL and the Edgware & Hampstead Railway Act was passed in 1902. Nothing very much was done about constructing the line until 1912 when the E&HR was absorbed by the LER. In the meantime some adjustments had been authorized to the proposed route, some areas of which were enjoying extensive housing development. Before war broke out the LER managed to purchase much of the land required for the extension and some preliminary work started.

Once the Trade Facilities Act was passed work proceeded immediately. Major contracts were placed in 1922 and work progressed very quickly with the extension opened as far as Hendon on 19th November 1923 and beyond to Edgware on 18th August 1924. Stations were provided at Brent (now Brent Cross), Hendon Central, Colindale, Burnt Oak and Edgware. From Golders Green to Brent the line was largely on brick viaduct, with one deep cutting, although with the exception of a cutting and a section of tunnel near Hendon there was little in the way of extensive earthworks on the remainder of the line. The tunnels north of Hendon were standard twin tube tunnels of 11ft 8¼ins in diameter driven by means of rotary excavators except for a portion beneath the London, Midland & Scottish Railway where some care was needed and the tunnel was dug by hand. All stations consisted of a pair of island platforms and a car shed for additional rolling stock was provided at Edgware. A reversing siding was located between the running lines just north of

Colindale was typical of stations on the Edgware extension of 1923–24 and was designed by the Underground Group's architect, Stanley Heaps. This particular station was severely damaged during the war and the booking hall and frontage was subsequently rebuilt to a new design. *source UERL official photograph*

Colindale; signalling was automatic and in the open air coloured light signals were installed. Signal cabins were required at Edgware, Colindale and Hendon. Provision was made at Brent for passing loops for 'non-stop' trains to overtake those in the platform. The loops and associated signal box were not commissioned until 1927 although the innovation was not long lived and they were taken out of use in 1936. A third platform at Edgware was added in 1932.

Stations were spacious and were generally of a neo-Georgian style faced with Portland stone, although Edgware was distinctly Italianate and was set back from the road to allow for a forecourt (for feeder bus services) which was flanked by a pair of colonnades. Burnt Oak was a more modest brick building reflecting the absence of promising traffic objectives at that time – even so, the station opened late, on 27th October 1924, owing to a builders' strike. A larger permanent building was opened in August 1928 when development in the area became extensive.

Considerable alterations were made at Golders Green where the entire track layout was remodelled and an additional platform face provided to allow trains reversing there to conflict as little as possible with the new through services. The substation was enlarged to share the supply to the extension with a new substation at Burnt Oak, which was remotely controlled from Golders Green. A further substation was opened at Hendon in 1930. The supply was taken from Lots Road generating station which had gradually been enlarged, although a few years later the Edgware extension was fed from a bulk supply provided by the Metropolitan Railway at Neasden.

A rare (and a posed) photograph of the C&SLR below ground prior to reconstruction. Taken at Euston, one of the later batches of locomotives is evident in the platform on the left and a train of the more recent rolling stock on the right. The entrance to the train through the gated platform between the carriages is clearly visible and may be seen to be a single vestibule between them, unlike the Hampstead cars where there were separate platforms on each car. The platform on the right now forms platform 6 at Euston (looking towards Camden Town). The other platform was removed in 1967.   *source M A C Horne Collection*

The acquisition of the C&SLR by the UERL in 1913 presaged very major reconstruction in order to transform its innovative but antiquated method of operation into something more in keeping with the UERL's approach. It had long been realized that the small, nonstandard tunnel diameter was unduly restrictive and would prevent the use of a standard type of rolling stock. Platform lengths were far short of prevailing standards and it was felt that an extension northwards to Camden Town with consequent through running on to the Hampstead Line's northern branches would take advantage of the spare capacity available.

The necessary powers were obtained in 1913 but apart from some experimental tunnel enlargement and extensive planning work little else happened for a further seven years. Deferring reconstruction during the war did not prevent some equipment modernization. When Stockwell power station closed in 1915, and power was taken from Lots Road, Hopkinson's 5-wire distribution system was abandoned and new substations were installed at Stockwell, Elephant & Castle and Old Street, with further power taken from the Hampstead substation at Euston which was enlarged; Angel and London Bridge substations were closed at the same time. Starting in 1919 the existing signalling equipment was replaced by a fully track circuited a.c. system similar to the UERL standard though without provision of trainstops – the locomotives were not fitted with tripcocks and 'assistant' drivers were still carried. The final section of new signalling, from Stockwell to Clapham Common, came into use on 1st January 1922.

Work on the extension from Euston to Camden Town also started in 1922, and to allow fast progress on tunnel enlargement the existing railway was closed between Moorgate Street and Euston from Wednesday 9th August that year. On the remainder of the line Borough (and later Kennington) closed to allow the platforms to be used as worksites as it was the intention to keep the railway in operation between Clapham and Moorgate Street while the reconstruction proceeded all around. For this purpose a shield was devised which allowed trains to pass exposed clay during the day at the worksites where the tunnels were being enlarged at night. To aid matters the railway was opened later in the morning with last trains leaving the termini at 7:14pm at night. An auxiliary bus service, run on behalf of the C&SLR, was operated along the portion of the line temporarily closed and stopping intermediately only at King's Cross, Angel, City Road and Old Street. From the start of 1923 this service was withdrawn and replaced by a new service operating along the whole of the line in order to relieve the congestion.

During the C&SLR reconstruction both Kennington and Borough stations were closed and converted into working sites. Engineers' trains for the tunnel reconstruction works were stabled in sidings on the former platform sites. Spoil was unloaded and new materials delivered via the former station liftshafts. Until the whole line was temporarily closed, passenger trains continued to operate through the stations non stop (in this instance, to the left of the wooden partition). *source UERL official photograph*

Stockwell depot became the principal worksite and base for numerous works' trains; spare stock and nine service trains were out-stabled in the tunnel north of Moorgate Street to make more room, although some spare coaches were stabled in a siding laid along part of the King William Street branch. Initially a two-minute interval service of 5-coach trains was operated but this became problematical with the number of speed restrictions and, later, areas of single line working south of Oval as the railway increasingly took on the appearance of a vast building site; the service latterly dropped back to four minute intervals. Towards the end of 1923 some 19,000 out of 22,000 tunnel rings had been enlarged, in many instances by re-using existing segments with additional key pieces, and work was proceeding at some sixty sites. At 5:12pm on 27th November 1923 railway traffic came to a dramatic end. At a point near Borough, where the existence of a sand and gravel portion was anticipated, special construction had just started to avoid disturbing the tunnel crown during enlargement. The extreme ends of special construction, where the ground was presumed safe, was to have been built for simplicity by temporarily removing the top segments as work progressed, as had been done elsewhere. The gap between the old and enlarged tunnels was secured by substantial boards with the ends wedged behind the segments, to hold back the clay. Unfortunately the exact position of the unsound ground was slightly misjudged, and after the second special ring had been built, and the gap between that and the next ring to be started had been boarded over, it was not realized that there was unsound ground immediately above the veneer of clay at this point.

The railway might have carried on unscathed had not one of the boards somehow become dislodged and dropped down to be hit by a passing train which disturbed the delicate status quo immediately above. The driver stopped the train and removed the wood from the line then the guard reported water and gravel coming into the tunnel near the back of the train. Fortunately the driver managed to extract the train and get it to Borough before the traction current went off. Within 15 minutes the tunnel was completely blocked by the inrush and in due course about 650 tons of gravel settled down to await removal. As a result of this subsidence a huge crater formed beneath Newington Causeway some forty feet above. Surprisingly the road surface remained undisturbed for about fifty minutes when a build up of gas beneath, where an unsupported gas main had failed, caused a huge explosion. The gaping hole thus uncovered remained alight from the ignition of escaping gas until an unsupported water main failed and put out the fire. Closed by force of circumstances the railway was not re-opened until reconstruction was completed.

The first section of the C&SLR to re-open was the portion from

Moorgate (the "Street" was dropped) to Euston and the connection with the Hampstead line at Camden Town. Through trains from Moorgate to Hendon were run from the outset on 20th April 1924. City Road station was permanently closed as traffic there had been very light. South of Moorgate the line was re-opened on 1st December 1924. At Euston the lifts (joint with the Hampstead Line) were retained as were those at King's Cross and Angel, which were modernized. At Bank the lifts were retained and modernized as were those at London Bridge, Borough, Elephant & Castle and Kennington. At the remaining stations it was decided to replace the lifts with escalators although (except at Stockwell) they were not completed at the time of re-opening and the old lifts were temporarily retained. It should be noted in passing that electric lifts had replaced the hydraulic lifts at the original stations before the First World War. In most cases escalators led from existing station superstructures although at Moorgate a new ticket hall was built at basement level and at Clapham Common a new station site was selected with the ticket hall beneath the roadway. Borough and Kennington stations, which had been worksites, were also delayed in opening. All platforms were modernized, retiled and extended from 200 to 350 feet (about 61m to 106·7m); at Stockwell the old single station tunnel was abandoned and replaced by twin platform tunnels immediately to the south. At Kennington and Elephant & Castle one of the platforms and the running lines were transposed to ease alignments. The surface buildings were generally modernized and re-used except at Clapham Common. After clearing up operations the depot at Stockwell was closed and sold, most of the locomotives were cut up and the rolling stock disposed of. New rolling stock was provided to furnish the C&SLR and Edgware extensions and from this point onwards the C&SLR and Hampstead Line of the LER were treated as a single entity although legally separate for several years more.

The junctions at Camden Town required extensive and complex construction work and when completed allowed trains from either route southwards to proceed to either route northwards, and vice versa, without conflict. The network of tunnels was built around the existing junction with almost no disturbance to traffic.

It should be mentioned at this point that South Kentish Town station did not survive to enjoy the advantages of the new services on the combined new railway. Located between Camden Town and Kentish Town, and not far from either, traffic had been very disappointing. It was one of a number of stations closed on 5th June 1924 because of a strike at Lots Road generating station but, unlike the others, it never re-opened.

Once the C&SLR reconstruction was in hand some further latent schemes received close attention. The increased capacity of the rebuilt line meant that it was now possible to consider seriously a southern extension from Clapham towards Tooting. The associated District Railway had had powers to construct a line from Wimbledon to Sutton, obtained in 1910 but not built. The UERL formulated a scheme to extend the C&SLR via Tooting and Morden and thence to Sutton by means of the Wimbledon & Sutton powers. However, the London & South Western – later Southern – Railway objected most strongly to what they considered to be an invasion of their territory and after some horse-trading they agreed not to oppose an extension to Morden if the UERL would transfer the Wimbledon & Sutton powers to the Southern. As an adjunct to the Morden extension it was further proposed to extend the southern end of the Hampstead Line from Charing Cross via Waterloo to Kennington, where there would be connections with the C&SLR to allow through running towards Morden. There was also a brief flirtation with a proposal for a network of junctions at Waterloo with the Bakerloo Line to allow innumerable possibilities of interworking; as part of the delicate negotiations with the Southern Railway this part of the scheme was, probably for the better, jettisoned.

Powers for the Clapham to Morden extension and the Charing Cross to Kennington link were granted in 1923 and preparations began immediately. Construction of the 5½-mile extension to Morden began at the end of 1923 and tunnelling was projected from a number of working shafts simultaneously with both rotary excavators and Greathead shields in use. At the height of activity twelve small shields and six large (station tunnel) shields were in use and serviced from eighteen shafts. Several portions of the tunnels had to be constructed under compressed air because of the water-bearing strata experienced. At Dorset Road, about half a mile north of Morden, the

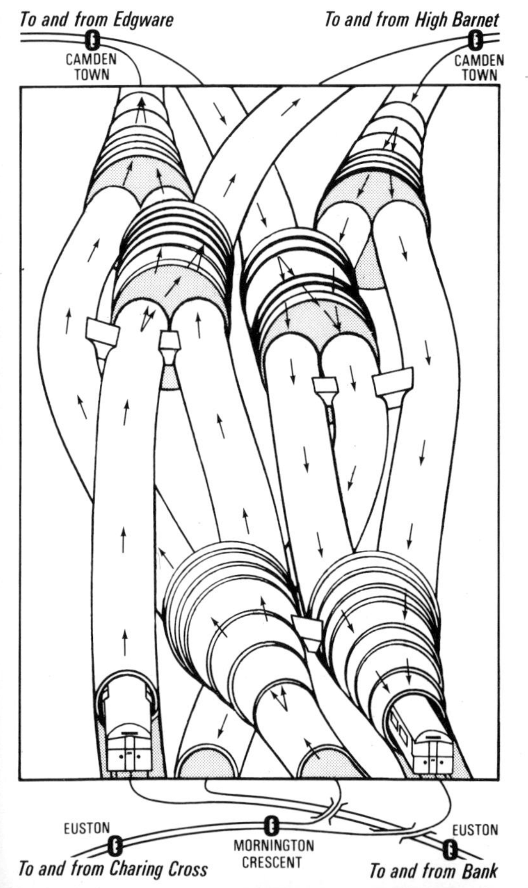

Arrangement of the tunnels at Camden Town junction after 1924

Originally to have been called Nightingale Lane, this station is typical of those provided on the Morden extension when it opened in 1926 and is based on a design by Charles Holden. A block of flats has subsequently been constructed above the wings.

source UERL official photograph

tunnels approached the surface and construction in open cutting was contemplated. However, the ground in the vicinity was found excessively water bearing and it was decided to build this portion of line in twin concrete tunnels built on the cut and cover principle. Gulleys were formed in the base of each tunnel which led to sumps at the tunnel mouth at Morden and at Dorset Road from both of which seepage water could be pumped away.

Morden station was in the open air and comprised three tracks and five platform faces. South of Morden twin tracks led to an extensive depot site with accommodation for 250 cars and room for further expansion – of which advantage was soon taken. Morden station was an impressive building faced in Portland stone and set back from the London Road to provide a lay-by for feeder bus services. A novel addition was the provision of a garage and car park opposite which was run as another UERL subsidiary and acknowledged the growing importance of the motor car.

Other stations were provided at Colliers Wood, South Wimbledon (which was really in Merton), Tooting Broadway, Trinity Road, Balham and Clapham South. All the stations were built to a similar theme with surface structures in Portland stone and with concrete canopies. The Underground group 'bullseye' featured prominently across the windows above the canopy. The style was conceived by Charles Holden and adapted at each site. Generally the booking halls were at street level and escalators led down directly to a concourse between each platform. At Balham and Trinity Road entrances at street level led to a booking hall below the street. Platforms were all similar and finished in the green and white tilework which charac-

Elevation of a 1926 stock car clearly illustrating the space occupied by the motor bogie and electrical switch compartment behind the cab. Only the centre double doorway was available for use by passengers (and this had a centre fixed pillar in the way); the hinged door at the trailing end was for the sole use of the guard.   *source UERL official photograph*

terizes all the stations built or modernized during this period.

Signalling was to the same standard as that on the remainder of the modernized C&SLR but signal cabins were installed only at Morden and Tooting Broadway, where there was a reversing siding.

On both the Morden extension and the reconstructed line train-stops were provided (as on the Hampstead Line) as the new stock was equipped with tripcocks. Power came not from Lots Road but was purchased in bulk from the County of London Electric Supply Company's power station at Barking. It was received at a switch house at Colliers Wood and fed to substations at South Wimbledon and Balham – the latter being remotely controlled from South Wimbledon. The new line was opened with appropriate ceremony by the Parliamentary Secretary to the Minister of Transport, Lieutenant-Colonel J T Moore Brabazon, on 13th September 1926, having been delayed by the industrial problems of that year; in fact Balham was still not quite ready and opened on 6th December.

The Charing Cross to Kennington link also opened on 13th September 1926, and created the complicated network of routes whereby trains from Morden could proceed either to Edgware or Highgate via either the Bank or Charing Cross. Although this final link was only about two miles long its construction did not fail to provide areas of problem. At Charing Cross the existing line was in the form of a loop and there was only one platform. Fortunately this was located in a position which allowed incorporation into the new northbound line and the necessary connection was made immediately to the south of the platform. On the southbound line the new track diverged from the old loop line just south of the Strand and ran into a new platform at Charing Cross. Beyond the platform the new southbound line pierced the loop line at an angle, rendering it unusable. In order to provide a service to Charing Cross between the time the loop came out of use and the new line was opened half the service reversed at Strand and the other half was projected to Charing Cross and back along the northbound tunnel on a single line working

Interior of a 1926 stock motor car looking towards the driving end. Among the roof advertisements the one to the far left advertises Morden Station Garage, run by the Underground Group and an early example of the promotion of 'rail heading' by motor car. It may be noted that the then current line diagram bore a perhaps unfortunate likeness to a snail, a point rudely made by a tongue-in-cheek cartoon in the staff magazine of the day!

source UERL official photograph

basis. The new platform was connected to a further enlarged station at Charing Cross by a pair of escalators and further stairways. Twin tunnels continued south of Charing Cross beneath the Thames to Waterloo and thence to Kennington where the tunnels spread out to flank the C&SLR station. Beyond, there were connections to the C&SLR although the extension tunnels continued to meet in the form of a huge reversing loop. In addition to these works a reversing siding was built between the two C&SLR running lines south of the station.

At Waterloo a bank of three escalators connected a new concourse situated between the new platforms and those of the Bakerloo with a new booking hall beneath the main line station – the existing Bakerloo lifts were retained. Power for the link was obtained from Lots Road via a new substation at Lambeth North (Bakerloo) station beneath which the new line passed.

Rolling stock for the new extension was generally similar to that provided for the C&SLR reconstruction and it is convenient to deal with these together. Between 1923 and 1925 new all-steel cars were constructed which incorporated air-operated doors under the control of two guards (and, later, one guard). 409 cars were provided, consisting of 181 Motor Cars, 100 Trailers and 128 Control Trailers. Construction of the new cars was divided between Cammell Laird, the Metropolitan Carriage, Wagon & Finance Company and the

Birmingham Railway Carriage & Wagon Company. In 1926 Metropolitan Cammell received orders for a further 64 motor cars and 48 trailers and in 1927 for a further 110 motor cars, 160 trailers and 36 control trailers. By this time the original Hampstead Line gate stock was something of an anachronism and was withdrawn early in 1929 on completion of delivery of the 1927 stock.

These new trains became collectively known as Standard stock. At first they operated in 5-car formations but this was soon increased to 6-car and from 1927 about half the service was operated in 7-car formations which arrangement prevailed for about ten years more. The motor cars continued the previous arrangement of solebar swept over the motor bogie, with the switch compartment above. During slack periods 3-car portions were uncoupled and stabled and the residue remained in service. As with the original stock all early deliveries were necessarily by road, this time to either Morden or Golders Green depots. However from March 1926 a single-line connection was constructed between the C&SLR and the Piccadilly Line at King's Cross which provided a physical connection with the rest of the Underground and thenceforth all stock transfers were made using this.

To cope with the increased traffic resulting from the extensions and improvements elsewhere several central London stations were improved. At Tottenham Court Road the lifts were replaced by escalators. Three escalators were constructed from the old Hampstead Line ticket hall to a new intermediate concourse which connected with the Central London Railway platforms, the old CLR ticket hall being closed; these came into use in September 1925. Two further escalators led from the concourse to the Hampstead Line platforms and these opened in February 1926. In April 1933 an additional escalator was provided between the concourse to a point half way along the Hampstead Line platforms. At Leicester Square lifts were dispensed with in May 1935 and a spacious new booking hall constructed beneath the road surface with a triple bank of escalators leading to a circulating area just above the Hampstead Line platform level, to which it was connected by stairs; further escalators led from the ticket hall to the Piccadilly Line. At Warren Street a new booking hall and escalators were provided in September 1933. Lifts were also dispensed with at Camden Town (October 1929), Highgate (June 1931) and Kentish Town (November 1932) where in each case a pair of escalators was installed, although the existing emergency spiral stairways were retained.

In 1933, after years of public debate, a new type of public authority came into being. This was the London Passenger Transport Board (LPTB), which on 1st July of that year took over the responsibility for all London's bus, underground railway and tramway services. A noteworthy factor was that the Chairman and Vice-Chairman of the new Board were no lesser individuals than Lord Ashfield and Frank Pick who had previously been Chairman and Managing Director, respectively, of the UERL. The headquarters of the LPTB was Holden's impressive 55 Broadway complex in Westminster which had previously been the headquarters of the UERL and constituent companies – whose staff in any case formed the bulk of the new LPTB employees. It is not surprising, therefore, that no major changes of policy happened very quickly. Nevertheless part of the justification for the new Board was the increased opportunity for further schemes of expansion, and plans were quickly formulated for a scheme of new works which took into account both the relentless expansion of London and the shortcomings of transport facilities in many existing areas.

The scheme became known as the 1935–40 New Works Programme. A significant element of this was that it was in the interest of the main line railway companies to co-operate with the scheme as a result of a statutory revenue pooling scheme between themselves and the LPTB which also came into operation with the formation of the new Board. The estimated cost of the scheme was £40,000,000 which was underwritten by a Treasury guarantee.

The joint Hampstead Line and C&SLR had, after effective amalgamation in 1924–26, become termed the Edgware, Highgate & Morden Line and then the Morden–Edgware Line and after a continued uncomfortable existence with this title was in 1937 renamed the Northern Line, which name it is convenient to use hereafter. The New Works Programme profoundly affected many of the Underground lines. The Northern Line's share of the programme was extensive. It envisaged an extension of the Highgate branch to the East Finchley station of the London & North Eastern Railway (LNER) which would be electrified northwards to High Barnet, including the branch from Finchley (Church End) – now Finchley Central – to Edgware. This latter branch was a single track line worked by a shuttle service and as part of the scheme it would be doubled. At Edgware the LNER line would be diverted into the existing Northern Line station which would be enlarged.

It is necessary to digress for one moment from the subject of the Northern Line in order to explain the circumstances of this LNER branch, since its later history is in fact integral with the Line. It started life as the Edgware & Highgate Railway and opened under the aegis of the Great Northern Railway (GNR) on 22nd August 1867. It ran from a junction just north of what is now Finsbury Park station to Edgware. Intermediate stations were initially situated at Crouch End, Highgate, East End (later East Finchley), Finchley & Hendon (later Finchley [Church End]), and Mill Hill (latterly Mill Hill East). Double track was laid only as far as Highgate when the branch opened, but was soon extended northwards to Finchley; beyond this point sufficient land was acquired for future doubling and the Dollis Viaduct was of sufficient width for two tracks. Between Crouch End and Finsbury Park a new station called Stroud Green opened in 1881, and between Edgware and Mill Hill a 'halt' was opened in 1906 called The Hale.

The importance of the single line to Edgware diminished significantly in 1872 when a further branch line opened. This ran from a junction immediately north of the platforms at Finchley to a station at High Barnet and was double track throughout with intermediate stations at Torrington Park (later Woodside Park) and Totteridge (now Totteridge & Whetstone). Subsequent housing development in rapidly developing Finchley in due course spawned the need for a further station at West Finchley (opened in 1933) and the LNER assembled a motley collection of odds and ends from elsewhere on its system for this purpose. The train service from London largely ran through to High Barnet and the Edgware service was relegated to a steam railmotor shuttle service from Finchley, where it had a platform for its exclusive use.

The following year, 1873, saw yet another branch spring into life. This branch left its forebears just north of Highgate (at a place known as Park Junction) and meandered into the grounds of the Alexandra Palace where a station was built cojoined to the Palace itself. Intermediate stations were opened at Cranley Gardens and Muswell Hill. In due course increasing traffic levels caused considerable embarrassment to the GNR (and later the LNER) because of the lack of capacity for the branch trains between Finsbury Park and King's Cross. The North London Railway and its successors helped out by allowing a proportion of these branch services to run to Broad Street via a connection at Canonbury, but by the mid 1930s travelling conditions south of Finchley and Muswell Hill had become wholly inadequate.

In addition to those railways, to the north of Finsbury Park, there existed the relatively unprosperous Great Northern & City section of the Metropolitan Line, which ran southwards from Finsbury Park to Moorgate via Drayton Park, Essex Road and Old Street. Opened in 1904 as the Great Northern & City Railway (GN&CR) and acquired by the Metropolitan Railway in 1913, the line ran in deep level tube for most of the way although Drayton Park was in open cutting and the car sheds were located alongside. As a further part of the New Works Programme it was proposed to construct a pair of ramps north of Drayton Park to bring the tube line to the surface. Here it was intended to run alongside the LNER to new platforms at Finsbury Park and then link up with the LNER branch line which would be electrified to Alexandra Palace and East Finchley, where it would

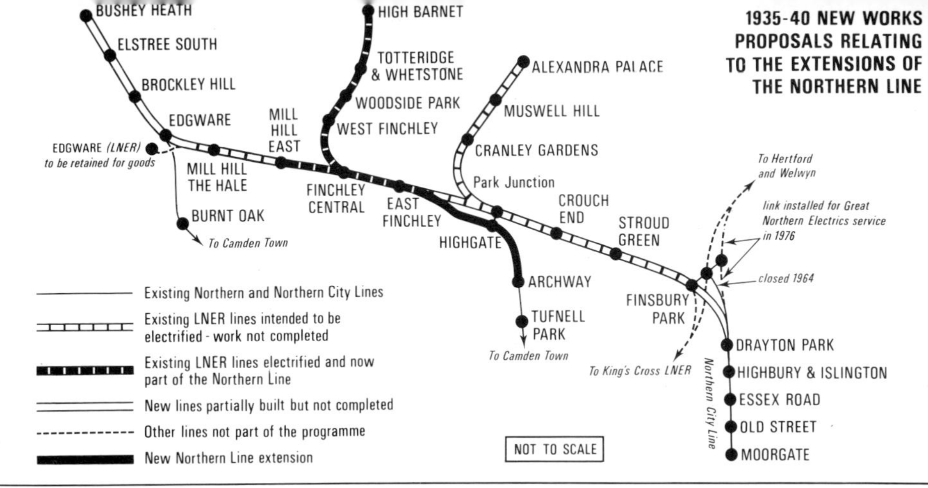

meet up with the Northern Line extension. As part of the programme the GN&CR section became, in effect, part of the Northern Line although within the LPTB it was usually called the Northern City Line.

A later addition to the programme was an extension of the Northern Line northwards from Edgware via new stations at Brockley Hill, Elstree South and Bushey Heath; a vast new depot was proposed between Elstree and Bushey to provide adequate stabling and maintenance facilities to service the new extension. Parliamentary powers were obtained in 1936 and 1937 and work started in earnest. North from Highgate one of the existing sidings was retained as a reversing point when the line was extended northwards. This station was eventually renamed Archway in December 1947 after a brief period of being called successively Archway (Highgate) and Highgate (Archway); it is convenient to use the name Archway hereon as the next station along the line was situated immediately beneath the LNER station called Highgate and took this as its name. Highgate LNER station was in deep cutting next to the Archway Road and a new ticket hall was constructed beneath the existing platforms with steps leading up. Escalators were installed between the new ticket hall and the new platforms 60 feet (18·3m) beneath. Steps led from the ticket hall to an entrance in Priory Gardens and to the former approach road which became a car park. Because of the steep rise to the Archway Road a further pair of escalators were to lead from the ticket hall to an additional entrance on the Archway Road, near the corner of Muswell Hill Road. North of Highgate twin tube tunnels continued on a steep rising gradient to emerge either side of the LNER tracks. East Finchley was completely rebuilt to provide four platforms. To the north there were adjustments to the track layout and to platform heights but the existing stations remained largely unchanged.

The high level (ex LNER) platforms at Highgate shortly before the British Railways Alexandra Palace branch closed. The new station canopy and waiting room, and the steps to the LT booking hall (beneath these platforms), can be seen at the far end of the platform, and an LT roundel sign is visible in the foreground. Had the New Works Programme been completed Northern Line trains from Moorgate via Finsbury Park would have passed through on their way to Alexandra Palace, High Barnet and Bushey Heath. Although conductor rail is not visible in this photograph, much was actually laid along this section of line. This view is taken looking north towards Park Junction (at the other end of the tunnels) and East Finchley.

source Photomatic Ltd

To provide sufficient trains for the various New Works extensions a large new fleet of rolling stock was purchased. The new trains took advantage of the latest advances in equipment design and incorporated a larger number of smaller motors than on previous trains; this enabled a neater type of motor bogie to be used which avoided the need for raised underframes at the leading end of the car. The control equipment consisted of a camshaft mechanism which cut out the traction resistances on starting, and was sufficiently compact to be accommodated beneath the floor. On motor cars these two new features made it possible to avoid the provision of special switch compartments, which increased the Motor Car passenger capacity by about a third and allowed a second double doorway to be added on each side. The new trains were known as 1938 stock and the total order consisted of 1121 cars, divided between Metropolitan Cammell and Birmingham Railway Carriage & Wagon Company Limited. Motor cars – now termed Driving Motor Cars – amounted to 644 and trailers, 251. The balance of 226 cars were of a new type called Non-Driving Motor Cars which were similar in design to trailers but with the addition of traction motors.

The new stock was, for the first time on tube stock, assembled into semi-permanent formations of three or four cars, each unit containing a Driving Motor Car at the outer ends and trailers and Non-Driving Motor Cars in between. The driving motor cars were equipped with a fully automatic coupler at the 'outer' end to allow push button coupling and uncoupling of all mechanical, electrical and air connections between units. Prototype driving motor cars were built in 1935/36 and tested on the Piccadilly Line; 18 of the 24 cars were constructed with streamlined driving ends but it was decided not to build the main batch of stock in this form.

To increase the carrying capacity of all the lines to be extended or improved it was decided to restock the Northern Line completely with the new trains; the displaced cars being re-allocated to the Central Line and Northern City Line. The balance of the new trains were to be used on the Northern City and Bakerloo Lines to make up the number required after they too had been extended. The first 1938 stock train entered service on the Northern Line on 30th June 1938 and the last Standard stock train ran in 1941. The old GN&CR rolling stock was withdrawn from the Northern City Line in August 1939 when Standard stock took over. Simultaneously current rail arrangements were revised to standard LPTB practice (previously on this line both positive and negative rails had been located outside the running rails).

The Northern Line was extended from Archway to East Finchley on 3rd July 1939 although the new Highgate station was unfinished and was not ready for opening until 19th January 1941. The new tube service connected with the existing steam services which temporarily shared the same platforms and then reversed north to south in temporary electrified sidings north of the station. At the same time the LNER line south of East Finchley was electrified to a point a little beyond Park Junction – almost a mile to the south – to allow tube stock to stable in Highgate carriage sidings.

On 14th April 1940 tube trains were projected northwards over newly electrified tracks to High Barnet where further siding accommodation was introduced. From the same date main line trains were withdrawn north of East Finchley. The layout of this station was completed at this stage with the main line trains using the inner platform faces of a pair of island platforms and the tube trains the outer faces. North of the platforms the main line tracks threw off connections to the north and southbound running lines and then combined to form a centre reversing siding – the main purpose of which was to accommodate the proposed off-peak Moorgate (via Finsbury Park) to East Finchley service when it was introduced. Signalling was controlled from new signal cabins at Park Junction, East Finchley, Finchley Central and High Barnet and although being of

A 1938 stock train entering the southbound platform at Woodside Park *circa* 1960. This station is fairly typical of those inherited from the LNER and the goods yard to the north of the station was still operational at this time (with goods traffic operated by British Railways). The goods yards all closed in the mid 1960s and station car parks were provided on the sites.

source M A C Horne Collection

the LPTB standard arrangement, was modified to allow the operation of LNER goods trains. Goods yards were retained at High Barnet, Totteridge, Woodside Park, Finchley Central, East Finchley and Highgate, for which purpose ground frames were provided for local shunting. Power was obtained from the North Metropolitan Electric Power Supply Company and distributed from a control room at East Finchley to new substations at High Barnet, Woodside Park, Finchley Central and East Finchley.

Shortly after war broke out the diversion of resources towards the war effort caused work to slow down on the remaining new works, and from June 1940 work virtually ceased. To allow work to proceed quickly on the doubling and electrification of the single line between Finchley Central and Edgware, the line had been closed completely in September 1939 and a substitute bus service provided between Edgware (LPTB) and Finchley Central, by way of Mill Hill (The Hale) and Mill Hill East; tickets were obtained from the railway ticket offices. To serve the barracks at Mill Hill East the railway was electrified on a single track basis from Finchley Central on 18th May 1941 when through tube trains began to operate. The state of the work beyond Mill Hill East did not allow electric trains to be projected further at that stage. The substitute bus service was cut back to Mill Hill East at the same time and in due course was replaced by an arrangement where LPTB rail tickets available between Mill Hill East and Edgware were accepted on bus route 240. Mill Hill (The Hale) ticket office was closed and the ticket stock transfered to Mill Hill Broadway (London Midland & Scottish Railway) station nearby. Some conductor rail installation and signalling work had been done, and Page Street substation building had been completed.

Although work had also stopped on the Bushey Heath extension the depot buildings at Aldenham were progressed rapidly and adapted for use as a temporary aircraft factory for the London Aircraft Production Group (some 710 *Halifax* aircraft were produced by London Transport between 1941 and 1945). After the war the factory was put to temporary use as a bus works to help recondition the ailing London bus fleet. Some of the earthworks on the remainder of this extension had been well advanced. Considerable work had been done at Edgware where a new substation and signal cabin had been commissioned, cuttings widened and sidings re-arranged. Part of a new route for the running lines to Burnt Oak were used for storage of spare or surplus rolling stock. Near Elstree part of some half-completed tube running tunnels were used as a Home Guard firing range.

Between Drayton Park and Finsbury Park extensive work had been done on the connections to bring the railway from tube level to that of the main line. However, work was suspended with only the south-bound ramp commissioned, and with the top temporarily connected with a siding in Highbury Vale yard to allow for stock transfers. The new Drayton Park signal cabin was also commissioned. Steelwork at Finsbury Park had been installed on the site of the proposed new platforms and north of the station much signalling work and conductor rail installation had taken place. Crouch Hill substation building had been completed. Some work had also been done on the Alexandra Palace branch. From March 1941 the LNER steam service into East Finchley ceased and the Alexandra Palace service dwindled into operation during peak hours only, interchange with the tube lines being via the escalator connection at Highgate. At this station work on the pair of high level escalators to Archway Road had been abandoned and one of the machines awaiting installation was soon used to replace war damaged equipment elsewhere.

Some central London stations were also modernized as a part of the New Works Programme, amongst which was King's Cross where in 1939 a new sub-surface ticket hall was opened to provide joint facilities for the Northern and Piccadilly Lines. New escalators led down to Piccadilly Line level then a further bank led down to the Northern Line level allowing the old C&SLR lifts to be dispensed with.

After the war the LPTB optimistically prophesied that work on the remaining New Works extensions would soon be completed, and future planning was made on this basis. Priority was given to the outstanding work on the Central Line extensions, which largely opened between 1946 and 1948, and the heavy restrictions on post-war capital expenditure prevented further moves on the Northern Line. In due course it was officially acknowledged that it was difficult to justify the heavy expenditure still required to extend the Northern Line across open countryside, through the Green Belt, to a barren crossroads at Bushey Heath. The main justification for this had been new depot accommodation but after more than five years of wartime operation without Aldenham it was difficult to argue convincingly now. The Bushey extension was officially dropped early in 1950 although the thought of reaching Brockley Hill lingered a little longer. Similarly extension from Mill Hill East to Edgware was noted as passing through thinly populated areas now unlikely to justify further expenditure, and this scheme, too, was abandoned. The single, unelectrified, line to Edgware remained until 1964 for goods services after which the track was removed. The 'replacement' through booking via bus route 240 became an increasing idiosyncracy until 1969 when the facility for through booking was finally withdrawn. To the end, stocks of Underground tickets, together with some 'Rover' tickets, were supplied to Mill Hill Broadway station and continued to be printed Mill Hill (The Hale). At one time season tickets were available on demand but from 1951 they were restricted to existing holders – from 1974 this facility, too, was withdrawn. The 'temporary' bus works at Aldenham which utilized the lifting shop and carsheds was rebuilt and made permanent in 1955.

The idea of extending the Northern City Line service northwards from Finsbury Park to Muswell Hill or Alexandra Palace lingered for some years, though nothing was actually done. After the reliability and comfort of the residual Alexandra Palace steam service had been allowed to drop to unimaginable depths of unattractiveness – including a two-month suspension at the end of 1951 – the passenger service was completely withdrawn from 5th July 1954, and with it any further thought of electrification.

From 1st January 1948 the LPTB was embodied into the scheme of nationalization of inland transport and was vested in the British Transport Commission. Most of the LPTB's operations were devolved to a new London Transport Executive and on the Northern Line the ex-LNER stations and lines north of Highgate were also vested with the LTE. At the end of 1964 the British Transport Commission ceased to exist and London Transport became a nationalized industry in its own right. From 1970 however, political control passed to the Greater London Council, then considered to be London's strategic planning authority.

With the stringent restrictions on post-war spending little opportunity existed for heavy capital expenditure and new works were largely confined to patching up war damage and minor improvements. In July 1948 a new interchange subway opened between the Piccadilly and Northern Line at Leicester Square, to relieve the existing tortuous, heavily used passages, though they were retained. The Festival of Britain in 1951 spurred improvements at Waterloo where a new bank of three escalators connected the low level concourse to the Festival site from May 1951. When the exhibition closed the escalators were retained, although one was replaced by a stairway when the machine was felt to be more use at Green Park. After temporary closure from 1957 to 1962 the escalator shaft was accommodated in a new ticket hall constructed beneath the new Shell building. The Festival of Britain was also the cause of two new escalators at Charing Cross, leading from the ticket hall to the sub-surface concourse below the District Line.

At Hampstead a pair of the old Otis lifts was replaced by two automatic high-speed lifts which came into service on 11th April 1954. This was the second high-speed installation on the Line, the first being at Goodge Street in 1937 when three automatic high-speed lifts were installed in a shaft previously occupied by two old lifts. At Highgate the moribund workings for the top flight of escalators were reconstructed and a single 'up' escalator was commissioned in August 1957 to carry passengers the further 60 feet from ticket hall level to the Archway Road; for payment of a small toll the escalator was also available for use by pedestrians.

The train service during the 1950s and 60s was provided by the fleet of 1938 stock. The fleet had been augmented by the addition of 91 cars (known as 1949 stock) which comprised trailers and a new type of car – the Uncoupling Non-Driving Motor (UNDM) which was a non-driving car but with facilities for shunting in depots and yards. These cars were needed to enable a grand sorting out of stock between the Piccadilly, Northern and Bakerloo Lines which created additional trains and mopped up the non-standard formations and the 18 experimental streamlined cars, which were rebuilt as trailers. The Northern Line allocation was 110 7-car trains, 46 of which included a UNDM car on the 3-car unit instead of a middle driving motor car. During the war years trains were operated as 7-cars all day but from November 1951 uncoupling of trains outside the peaks was introduced to save car mileage and both 3-car and 4-car trains operated – the former via the City and the latter via Charing Cross. After modification of the stock 'passenger door control' (where passengers could open doors under the overriding supervision of the guard) was introduced in April 1950 in open sections of line. After operating complications became an irritation both uncoupling and passenger door control were abandoned within ten years.

On the Northern Line signalling methods had evolved little beyond the system introduced with the opening of the CCE&HR in 1907, although the moving-spectacle signals had given way to two-aspect coloured light signals between the wars. Following experiments with remote control of signal frames, Camden Town was re-signalled for control by Interlocking Machines in September 1955. Three machines were provided: one at Mornington Crescent and two at Camden Town itself, one each for the northbound and southbound lines. The machines were under the overriding control of a push button control desk at Camden Town, although for normal purposes the train's route was selected automatically from the coded electrical descriptions passed between the other signal cabins.

A further development was the automatic working of junctions by programme machines, where the timetable was reproduced on a plastic roll in the form of punch holes so that routes were set up 'to programme' and signals cleared accordingly; a refinement was the incorporation of a clock mechanism so that certain train movements could be set up at the specific times required by the timetable. The first installation of programme machines was at Kennington in January 1958 where six machines were introduced. Further programme machines were installed at Camden Town in June and superseded the push button desk and train description control. Euston (City line) followed in November.

To supervise the programme machines a central control room was built in a disused lift shaft at Leicester Square, where a track diagram of the whole of the central area of the Northern Line was provided and on which the positions of all trains were indicated. Facilities were provided to monitor the programme machines and to intervene to route trains by push button as occasion demanded. In combination with the introduction of a central control room, the little used signal cabins at Charing Cross, London Bridge and Moorgate were closed and modified for remote, push button operation from Leicester Square. In due course the influence of the centralised control room extended southwards to Morden and northwards to East Finchley. Programme machines were introduced at Archway, East Finchley, Tooting and Morden, and the signal cabin at Clapham Common became remotely controlled from Leicester Square (the sidings and signal cabins at Angel and Stockwell were closed). In 1961 interlocking machines and a push button desk were introduced at Golders Green, which also took over remote control of Hampstead. In 1964–5 programme machines were introduced at Edgware and Colindale, with supervision from Golders Green.

When the Victoria Line was opened in 1967 a purpose-built control room was constructed at Cobourg Street, Euston, and space was reserved for future accommodation of the Northern Line. Between

1969 and 1976 programme machine supervision and centralized control was transferred from Leicester Square and Golders Green control rooms to Cobourg Street, and the signalling at Golders Green, High Barnet and Finchley Central was converted to programme machine control. This left Park Junction as the sole remaining signal cabin on the line – and this with only a few shunting moves to the depot a day, the junction having been removed in 1958 when the British Railways goods service on the Alexandra Palace branch ceased.

The construction of the Victoria Line necessitated an interesting diversion of the northbound line at Euston to allow same level interchange between the Victoria Line and the Northern Line City branch, which still used the narrow island platform in the single station tunnel inherited from the City & South London regime. A 2500 feet (762m) diversion tunnel was built starting just west of the connection with the Piccadilly Line at King's Cross and reconnecting with the existing northbound line to the north-east of Euston. A new northbound platform was provided on the diversion line when it opened in June 1967 following which the former island platform was served only by southbound trains and the disused trackbed filled in to allow the platform to be widened. The remainder of the station was reconstructed in stages with a new ticket hall coming into use in March 1965 and the lifts being withdrawn from service when the northbound line was diverted.

The Victoria Line demanded minimal alterations at Warren Street where access passageways were added to the existing arrangement at intermediate level and a third escalator replaced the centre stairway of the upper flight. At King's Cross the existing sub-surface ticket hall was considerably enlarged and a further pair of escalators added which led solely down to the Victoria Line; there was little other change at low level. At Stockwell on the Brixton extension the new platforms flanked the existing Northern Line platforms. A fixed stairway and a third escalator were provided to supplement the existing pair, and the ticket hall was entirely replaced by a modern, larger structure on a similar site.

Little other gratuitous building work took place during this period but mention should be made of a new ticket hall at Colindale, opened in 1962, which replaced a temporary structure erected following war damage, and Elephant & Castle where a new station building was provided in 1965 on the existing site, although the old lifts were not superseded until 1983.

During the late 1960s the reliability of the 1938 stock began to fall as the trains started to approach the end of their useful life. It was therefore decided to purchase some 30 new trains based on the Victoria Line 1967 stock design to allow the more unreliable cars to be scrapped and for the various non-standard cars (not just on the

1959 stock train between Finchley Central and Mill Hill East, looking towards the latter. In the background may be seen the convergence of tracks to form the single line which, a little beyond the points, is carried across the Dollis Brook on viaduct. On the left may be seen the remains of a former goods yard.   *source M A C Horne*

Northern Line) to be disposed of. These trains became known as the 1972 Mark I stock, the first new trains coming into service on 26th June 1972 and the remainder following over the next eighteen months. Each 7-car train consisted of one 3-car and one 4-car unit. The latter comprised a Motor Car at each end, each with four traction motors, and a pair of trailers in between. The 3-car unit comprised two Motor Cars and a single trailer, however one of these Motor Cars was an UNDM and was similar to the 1949 stock UNDMs whose shunting control cabinets were stripped out for re-use on the new trains. The 1972 stock was notable for its absence of side cab doors which was a feature of its Victoria Line origins where automatic operation was in use.

Before all the Mark I trains were delivered it was decided to purchase a further 33 trains of similar (but not identical) design for temporary use on the Northern Line to allow more 1938 stock to be scrapped – it was the eventual intention that these would be used on what is now known as the Jubilee Line. The first of these trains came into use on 19th November 1973.

The next stage in the replacement of the 1938 stock took place on 2nd December 1975 when a train of 1959 stock entered service, having been displaced from the Piccadilly Line by new trains there. Further transfers of stock from that line completely displaced the 1938 stock, the last service train running on 14th April 1978, although that did not prove to be the end of the story. Five 1938 stock trains re-entered service on the Northern Line from September 1986 as a temporary measure after being kept in store when withdrawn from Bakerloo Line service in 1985.

The 1972 Mark II trains were gradually withdrawn from the Northern Line for use on the Bakerloo and Jubilee Lines, the last one on the Northern Line being withdrawn in 1986. The Northern Line presently operates with a mixture of 1972 Mark I, 1959 and (temporarily) 1938 stocks. Complete re-stocking is not envisaged until the end of the century.

The construction of the Jubilee Line began in 1972 and involved major work at the proposed southern terminus at Charing Cross. An objective of the new scheme was to clear up the irksome turn-of-the-century anomaly whereby the Northern Line's Strand station and the Bakerloo Line's Trafalgar Square station were an almost literal stone's throw away from each other but were otherwise not connected. The new station was therefore planned to absorb Strand and interconnect with Trafalgar Square, the whole complex becoming known as Charing Cross. The new ticket hall was based on the former Strand sub-surface ticket hall, but was very considerably extended in area beneath the Strand itself and incorporated new subways to entrances in Villiers Street, Strand (north side) and William IV Street. The existing entrance from the main line station was retained although a single (up) escalator was added.

A major problem arose in providing access from the new ticket hall to the Northern Line platforms immediately below, where the existing service was provided by lifts. The most convenient arrangement of escalators required the upper flight to pass through the existing lift shafts which would have made it difficult to operate the station while the work was being done. The close proximity of Charing Cross (now Embankment) station invited the decision to close Strand station while the reconstruction work was being done, and thus the last train called on 16th June 1973. The reconstructed station came back into service (as Charing Cross) for the opening of the Jubilee Line on 1st May 1979, and on the same day the Northern Line platforms were restored to use and the Bakerloo Line station was renamed and linked to the Northern and Jubilee Lines. The Northern Line platforms had been completely redecorated, the basis being huge murals running the length of the platforms and portraying a design by David Gentleman of the construction of the medieval Charing Cross.

This re-arrangement effectively caused the Northern Line station to revert to the name it had originally borne when it opened in 1907; since the station served Charing Cross main line station it was eminently more appropriate in this guise. However it now became necessary to rename the station of the same name 400 yards (366m) to the south. To get passengers used to the new scheme of things Charing Cross (Northern, Bakerloo and District Line station) was renamed Charing Cross (Embankment) on 4th August 1974 and Embankment on 9th September 1976.

Throughout the Northern Line escalators had been introduced at all stations on the various extensions built after 1907 and had also

1972 Mark I stock train between Brent Cross and Golders Green.   *source M A C Horne*

superseded lifts at most of the busier stations. A large number of escalators had thus been introduced in the 1920s and 1930s which meant that by 1970 a very large proportion of escalators on the line were becoming life expired. A major programme of escalator modernization commenced in 1976 and ten years later the majority of escalators on the line had been superseded by more modern machines. At eleven stations access was still by means of lifts, with in nearly all cases the equipment dating back to the opening of the line in 1907 (and C&SLR lifts modernized in the 1920s largely utilized secondhand ex-LER equipment). Inevitably these lifts, though extremely rugged, were also beginning to show their age and a programme of lift replacement began, Angel and Chalk Farm being the first stations to receive new lift installations, both coming into use in 1979.

The post-war capital expenditure restrictions, which so far as public transport was concerned drifted on until the 1960s, left a legacy of dowdy and partially unkempt stations which were increasingly considered to be sufficiently unattractive to be affecting traffic. Initially a major programme of relighting stations to higher standards began, replacing tungsten filament bulbs with fluorescent tubes, most stations being tackled between 1974 and 1980. During the late 1970s it was realized that passengers placed rather greater weight on an attractive environment than hitherto had been thought. London Transport had been in the fortunate position under Greater London Council control to obtain considerable support for

46

capital expenditure and during a lull in purchases of very expensive new trains decided to switch this support towards a massive programme of station modernization and refurbishment. Under this programme most stations received at least a coat of paint and general clean up and the major stations were extensively modernized. Charing Cross had already been modernized as part of the Jubilee Line scheme and in the mid 1980s major work was undertaken at Tottenham Court Road, Leicester Square, Embankment, Waterloo, Goodge Street, Euston and King's Cross, with work planned at other sites. Moorgate and Old Street had already been improved in the late 1960s as part of other schemes and were similar in style to the contemporary Victoria Line. The later programme, however, was based on the premise that stations needed their own individual identity and striking new styles of design were employed.

When the component railways of the Northern Line were built ticket offices were such that the ticket windows were along one wall of the booking hall. During the 1920s it became the practice to install free-standing ticket offices, known as Passimeters. However, by the early 1980s many of these old offices no longer matched modern standards for working conditions or security, and as part of a new systemwide ticket issuing system new or reconstructed offices are being provided at every station. The new offices are all of the 'wall' type and many involve additional major reconstruction or re-arrangement of the booking hall areas.

The complexity of the railway resulting from the amalgamation of the LER and C&SLR in 1924 created a need for prior knowledge of the destination of the next few trains and at most stations where divergent routes lay ahead platform signs were installed to indicate the destination of the next two or three trains. These signs remained largely unaltered for over fifty years but as part of the philosophy of providing more information a new type of indicator was devised. This was an electronic indicator incorporating a 'dot-matrix' and could display any message it was given, unlike the older indicators which could only show what was painted on the glass. Linked to a computer the indicators could also show how long passengers would have to wait for the trains, and the times counted down as the trains approached. The initial installation was made at stations along the busy Charing Cross branch in 1982 and were later installed along the rest of the line.

In the early 1980s a slightly reduced operating fleet allowed certain changes to be made in the Highgate area. After inheriting carriage sheds from the LNER nine double-ended sidings (eight under cover) were available for stabling tube stock when the Northern Line was extended from East Finchley to Finsbury Park and became known as Highgate Depot. There was also a separate group of four electrified sidings which were adjacent to the Alexandra Palace branch. Although this site was intended to accommodate double-ended running sidings, only lightly laid 'temporary' sidings were actually installed for use during the electrification works. Shortage of stabling accommodation soon caused them to be used for service trains and during latter years five trains were stabled there. Highgate Wood sidings were closed in 1981 and the trains dispersed elsewhere. Highgate Depot was closed in 1984 and Park Junction signal box was abandoned at the same time. While the future of the site was considered the depot and approaches remained in situ and two sidings were available for engineers' trains. With passenger business increasing in the late 1980s the possibility of re-opening the depot is being considered.

In the meantime the control of the Northern Line had also changed. On 10th July 1984 the London Transport Executive passed from Greater London Council control to that of the Secretary of State for Transport under the Transport Act of that year, the body also being restyled London Regional Transport. Under a provision of the Act a subsidiary company was established on 29th March 1985 called London Underground Limited and on 1st April 1985 London Regional Transport's railway activities passed to this subsidiary company.

The Northern Line has thus developed from crude, pioneering beginnings to one of the largest of the deep level tube lines. It incorporates the longest continuous tunnel on the London Underground of 17¼ miles, from Morden to East Finchley via the City; until recently this was the longest railway tunnel in the world. The confidence of the promoters of the old City & South London Railway in an age when even electric light was still something of a novelty can only be admired, but it is doubtful even if they could have foreseen the impact that their little railway was to have in spawning new schemes and hence in moulding the future shape of London. Most passengers simply use the line to get from one place to another without a thought for how struggling miners toiled in unbearable conditions to build this, adapt that or reconstruct the other. Nor are they worried about how it was that engineers, probably working by the light of oil lamps, nearly a hundred years ago, managed to build tunnels from different points in London which weeks or months later would meet to within an inch!

In a book such as this it would be impossible to say anything about the mishaps which occur in any railway environment, or about the staff who have worked and run the railway for the last hundred years or so, or of the many other matters surrounding the circumstances of the Line. If, however, it has provided a brief insight into the general history of the Line it will have achieved its purpose.